FANTASY IN EVERY KEY

Also by Donny Barilla

GALAXIES IN THE RAINDROPS – Poems

DANCE UPON THE FOREST FLOOR – Poems

VANISH TO THE MOUNTAIN SPRING – Poems

GOING HOME – Poems

WINTER ON AN AUTUMN DAY – Poems

PATIENCE WITH EACH ROTATION OF THE EARTH
– Poems

I FOLLOW HER INTO THE SHADOW – Poems

Fantasy In Every Key

A collection of poems

by

DONNY BARILLA

BOOKS

Adelaide Books
New York / Lisbon
2020

FANTASY IN EVERY KEY
A collection of poems
By Donny Barilla

Published by Adelaide Books, New York / Lisbon
adelaidebooks.org
Editor-in-Chief
Stevan V. Nikolic

For any information, please address Adelaide Books
at info@adelaidebooks.org
or write to:
Adelaide Books
244 Fifth Ave. Suite D27
New York, NY, 10001

ISBN: 978-1-952570-54-4

Printed in the United States of America

to,

Sarah S.

"You shine through darkness."

Contents

Looking into the shimmer and glancing water;

Winds tug upon my moisture, resting on these freshest of dreams.

Rising Upon the Earth

The bed, a heavy banquet, I slip and smother each edge
as the pillows of soft down fed me in the sweats
in which she shuddered and soaked every satin sheet.

With the painted wine grapes, fullness of the merlot
we slip against. I flood my breath and sweetly smell
the rich blossom of the earth.

Powders, soft flours upon the doughs, these rising
and declining breasts enrich the swooning caress
of each nimble finger and each kneading lip.

Slithering across the juices and sweet suckling syrups,
I find myself alone in the dense groves of the woods.

Gentle, my hands slip, smooth their way across the damp,
well perched mosses which angle from tree to pebbled path.

Standing, I slowly surrender and walk through the ancient
multitudes of trees and thickets and shrub.

Undressing

I dismantle to the thrash and crackling moans
of the earth which deepened me to the
basin floor of the pasture.

I roamed alive in this grotto where we would shred each
thick wool and parcel of cloth.

I wrapped myself along the cool paints of pink and heavy peach.

Closer to the earth, I dipped my way
through the field where grasses
stood high and slithered against the calves and ankles.

I sat quietly on the wood bench as the
warm sky tangled through me.
Sweet moisture and smacking rain tamped.

There wrapped miles of threads
between us as I spread my lips
against the tremors of hers.

I left this feverish place as I smelled her
in the deep of this caked earth.

I angle my face to the blossom of the moon,
by morning, all petals of the orchids sweetly undress.

After the Closeness She Vanished

In the darkest moment of night, she slowly walked
through the glen, punishing me with
her fullness and her nakedness.

Shadow on shadow, the sycamore tree
drenched with long arms and
flung crimping leaves which lay soft under the newest moon.

I reached for her as the dusts and snapping
pods silently spoke of renewal
with the trimmed hour of the sun and
spoke of how the piercing rays
stung and stapled through each inch and
edge upon my wine colored flesh.

As I stood upon the soft minerals of the soil, I
shed coddling tears and returned my
watchfulness to her aromas and spices
which perched upon the mint and sweet sauces of the pine.

Along with this gentle breeze, I felt her
breath into my flickered hair.
She vanished with the openness of the splash of morning.

On Account of Summer

I am Summers breath which flickers the proud length
of the well cared for grass field.

I touch the sleek, moisture of your cheek, lips.
I feel the floods of the surmounting Summer storm.

You shake as the rapids of the quickest stream.
Pulling you aside as the unfastening buttons on your blouse;
I am the threads which loosen as you drip across me
in syrups and saps.

There roams a smash of a thick, warm storms;
I witness this with the fallen clouds deepen under the summit
of the towering peak.

Your eyes flicker in golds and white golds.
Through you, I witness the fields of rye as they motion
from neck to navel, freckled chest to blossomed breasts.

Wooded Grass Hut

I stepped my way through the open
dome of the muscling treetops.

Stepped quietly into this realm of
sanctuary, a quivering leaf scuffles
as a token, charm.

This forest seemed endless. This forest
quivered into the discipline
where the softest bend in the wood hushed and offered drink.

Lost and calm, I found a lavender bush
cloaked and trimmed with
a roaming bed of clover.

The grass hut overlooked the farthest spread and groom
where the valley trembled, coddled with the patterns;
The farmers field sulked in the heaviest coat of tan.

I rest and by the translucent perch of the sweetest pearl
which rest upon the wooded hut coated with grasses.

With winds abreast, I walk myself
through the oldest sky and yield
to the fever of this sunken Autumn day.

I Wait By Ocean

I look to your lips, slow perch these apricot skies.

Slightly apart, I feed upon an endless ocean.

Tender and coated in sweat, the gauze and cottons
Of your soaked t-shirt slopes in a slender pronouncement
Of the bashful softness where you grip the aroma.

The brine clings to you in threads and passions
Of the curving motions.

Thousands of prisms glimmer along the fever of this saddle,
Soft and slippery, the rest slants upon the vasts
Emptiness where we soothe, by rock and by breath.

Search

I slept through the hours when the walls, ceiling screamed.
With heavy sorrow, the lavender bush sank tender aromas
and pronounced the sods and muscles of the well spread
earth.

I begged for exchanges of the scent of
the breast and the garden
which tossed the tug of the heaviest mulch.

I weathered the denim and wools and walked through the dredge
and sorrow of the meadow from which I slumber and awaken.

With the snap of a quick grab of air, motherly breath,
I walk upon these hills and deepen through these fields.

I reach the ground covering of the well
spread patch of sweet mint.

Here, I lay across this coat of Spring grooming pastures.

So feverish, I find my way into the forest, most distant
on the other side of the roaming pine hills and cliffs.

There shot a sting, a roaming pierced echo which fractured
fast and eager to the crest of my well angled face;
I turned to the east and threaded upon
the path I once dearly lost.

Evening at the Pond

Asleep, the pond wavered and stroked
the blossom of the moon;
I stood and wiped dry the sting of my feet.

Sweet and tenderly, she stood from the basin, soft channel.

I lathered my eyes and watched her full walnut hair
cascade across her slippery shoulders. I witnessed
the majesty of her nakedness and full swelling groom
of the kelp which gripped to her ankles and feet.

Kissing her, I bloomed in the countless
fragrances she breathed.

Her nearest garden which flooded across me, softly
with gliding moisture which shot fluidly through the air,

I placed her cool trembling body upon mine.
Wrapped in garments and denim and
wools, I wiped the sleek film
upon my cottons and guided her to the patio
which strangled in eaves.

Looking to the threads of pale candle light,
I smiled upon the tears of wilt and dripped from the wax.
Oceanic Breast

I opened to the cool ocean winds,
softly, each shell and pebble angled beneath my feet.

Into the deep, I reached and found
the sweet grip of the kelp, lurking within the cove.

Upon the warm glaze of the sun,
I witnessed her pause and paints which flooded
into the prisms of my tender eyes.

Reaching, tossing the slated rock, tucked in the soft
beds of sand; I threw, dashed the fracture of the earth.

I returned this piece of antiquity upon the blossoming
oceanic breast.

Pulse of Morning

The heavy, thick sky flooded in grays,
flooded in marbles which dredged the flesh,
the salts of the earth.

With my head leaned back, I drank the spirits of this
blossomed touch.

⁓

I sank in the moisture of the plentiful bounty;
I softly spoke to the tremoring glaze
which soaked upon my floods,
openings of the cultured soil and mud.

⁓

Well into the brisk fractured slice of morning,
I touched her in the slight fever of smoothed daylight.

I am the leisure of her flesh and opened breasts.
together, I soften the pulsing warmth of her blood.

Pond

The sauces of the gathered richness of the pond
swept and coddled the edge and smoothness of my
most tender feet, suckling sweetly into the earth
as I lay beneath the soft dash of a gentle breeze.

I lay my face against the freckled chest which threaded
through and along the maps where I found
the treasures of your warm creams.

I watched you disrobe and remove every stitch
of your garment.

With an endless slice into the moaning sluice of the pond,
I reached into the walnut groove of your hair,
so alive with washed beads of water and tangling scents
where the cherry trees guarded as a sentinel.

Peak and Joust

Cluttered in stones and cast threw with chipped pebbles,
I climbed this trail as the thick raindrops
slapped upon the clays
and stiff, jagged muds.

Now, alive in the earliest fraction of this tender Spring,
I open my mouth and lungs and breath swift the fragrances
of this pine coated and evergreen mountain.

I hear the screams of the slapping, waters, which wash
and nurture each maddened craze of the dry postured
roots.

I stand as witness to the previous.
White flakes remain frosted, frozen
in the ice of my thick hair,
chestnuts of every strand and every hue which pattern across
my shoulders and neck.

Upon reaching the peak, this joust upon the mountaintop,
I breath this thinned, grasping threads of air.

I can feel the fog licking my ankles and feet.

Peach

I tangle with the warmth beneath your flesh.

Like fog across a meadow, you softly grazed
through to my aching, alabaster bones.

With sweats and the breadth of these wool blankets,
I soaked upon your most delicate fragrance.

Calling upon every moan of every purr sweeping
from the deep of my lungs and wisping
from the threads across my lips,
I sulked with this choir which meshed as we touched.

Stepping through the meadow of the wrangling hour
when sauced beads of the flicker of heaven
glazed into the wedge of my feet, I cupped your palm upon
the width of my hand.

So slowly, I wilted to the angles of a dying peach.

Eulogy in the Treetops

Gingerly, I traced pirouettes across the entangled greens,
Sweetly alive on this moist, forest floor.

In rhythms, the treetops cracked and shouted as the canvases
Broomed with the northern air.

As blood from the mountain spring, I drank swift.
Quietly, I sat by the veins of this endless, evergreen wood.

Here, I sleep as I always sleep.

I remove my fabrics of night and pause every moment.
Eagerly, I smell the blood beneath the forest soil.

I lurk to the face of the mountain cliff
As I have vanished in the fading
Spreads of deep Autumn.

Fangs of Spring

Walking in the mists of this silk, sleek blossomed grove,
I breathed the aromas of this flesh bearing apple tree,
curved and carved in red skins as I snapped into the width
of this juiced and moaning earth.

I recall the way the breasts of your soothing meadow
would lure and entice me to the fabrics
of the falling garments.

As I leaned upon the gnarled stalks of the budding branches,
I looked upon the swabbing fogs and fell to the lavish
legs as they crossed and gripped me in
the host of this burning groin.

Prior to the threads of winds so soft and the mumbling
glaze of the soaking grasses and earth, I lulled into the fabrics
of the thick sweet fangs of Spring.

The pale eggshell wash of the most tender blue,
each flickering cloud spread and I took to the grip of slumber
and faded along the mumbling swift winds.

Calmly, I return to the flesh, born of the earth.

Milks and Creams From This Mothering Sky

As I listen to the crimped, curled leaves,
I watch the acorn deepen in this mound.

The sky swelled and gathered rain from every damp
passing cloud.

On the brink of nightfall, I soothe to the fabrics and threads,
tumbling across the chisel of the earth.

I rest upon this stretched and roaming tree.

From branch to branch, I heard the
crackling moisture and pasture
where the smallest of buds shouted in glory.

Sap and Pines

The village slouched at the bottom reach
of the southern mountain.
This climb, shedding in leaves of brown and red
moaned with every step of my feet, wrapped in tight leathers.

Upon the peak of the sloping crest, filled with furs, I drank
from the sauces of the pouring spring and grew weary,
slept.

Leagues and leagues from my home, I awoke and shook
beneath the giggling, shedding gathering
of leaves which gripped
upon me as a blanket, coarse like burlap.

In a vast moment, I walked the well paved street.
Turning for a last glance, I smiled upon
the wide spread carpeting
of pines and the grip of winds which
pass by, moans of the sweet
crumbling marrow.

I still smell the pine and it's sap, swift winds.

Waiting For Nightfall

With webs and veins, I open this palm
and explore the universe.

Into the dampness of my weary contours,
from neck to the tundra of this
Loose and fine hair,
I sulk upon you and witness the bloods
of your torso and chest
Saturate the crisp, frigid dip of the sky.

With the endless meadows flooding across the valley, I
Tuck you in the cave of my humid mouth.

I lay upon the bloom of the carpet, heaviest greens.
You slouch and point to the tremble of the North star.

Through Night and Morning Return

There spread a glaze upon the morning grass;
swiftly, the black winged bird took flight.

With the tamp of my thick boot, I
snapped and crunched the clover, fallen sticks.

Leaning my ears to the threshing patterns of the timely sky,
I sulked beneath the graze and floods of the black and gray
clouds which took me in rhythms.

I removed the thin cotton shirt and bathed.
There cracked a snap and thrash in the deepest hour of night.

With swollen flesh and a cloak, the
fallen sky, sweeping across me
as I pressed against the floods of the deep.

Back to the hour of first light, I took to the path
and drank the sweetest pulps of apples and mint leaves.

Dying Voices

Upon the earth the leaves flutter and proclaim voices.

I return to the clamor of the rain as each drop, dashed
about the pale, softness of my face.

With the pale, sleek, pastes upon the cottons and her sweet
flesh, I removed the cloth and garments she wrestled against

I held her in the closeness as the shuffle
of each leaf upon each
neighboring earth.

Walking through the cluttered field of trees, I
felt each pulse of the thickened, deepened root.

Well into the deep of Autumn, I
treasured the naked branches
and I cherished her in all her full bodied dampness,
paying homage to each soft touch of flesh.

Resting by the Cove

This rowboat sliced through the cool,
chill of a heavy, deep water.
I paused upon the low rocks, slippery and
moistened with kelp and moss.

I turned to you and threaded my
humid breath upon you. Alive
with every spot of sweat and paste of
your fine hair which stuck
to the temples which call to me.

Aside from the bloods of these waters, I rest here with you.
I gather the crisp dashing water and
remove myself, only to flounder
upon you in the warmth of your flesh and pronouncement.

Winter Night and the Frozen Driftwood

Winter caressed the forest and earth
with the thin veils and gowns.
I paused by the slithering stream and
faintly I heard the voice,
the mothering threads of each rapid which fed and smoothed
each shard of trembling ice.

She came to me in the dance of a midnight hush.
Patterned in the dome, I soaked beneath
the frozen bloom of the velvet,
navy sky.

She asked me to touch her in the rhythms of the softest palm.
Pouched filled with her creams and milks, I
slipped the fresh touch of my lips against her and sweetly,
lay my cheek against her fabrics and lace.

In an instant, I look upon the dampest
slapping course of water.
By the grip of the driftwood, I paused my way and slowly
deepened through the heaviest chills of this Winter night.

Leaf

Here, I rest on the summit of Blue Mountain.
Every stone signs to me in choirs and calls to me in preludes.

Breathing the thin air, I rest upon the sleek, flat stone, slab.

I stand at this moment, tomorrow,
and a leaf from the sycamore
falls upon the bareness of my shoulder.

Dusts From the Treetops

I breathe the stitches of the earth, softly
each flickering weed and twig
moans sweetly as the damp threads of each patch of moss.

With the passages of this heavy wind,
I crumble with the shattered,
most gathered a mound of leaves.

With the rise of the burning sun, I shed this coat of dust.
Quietly, I step to the path and walk so tender, I collect each
aroma as they thresh from the wavering treetops.

Held in Each Goblet

From the skyward dome, I caught the pattern
of the sauces which dash and spread upon my palm,
the smoothest of goblets.

By the fracture of each moment of the next day,
I removed each fabric of our clothing.

Now, deep in the fields which shout of trembling
spear of jousting grass, I open as a cavern which cups
every hold of each slice of watery breath.

I wrap you in the thick flesh of my arms.
by nightfall, I walk you to your home.
Each groomed and fixed
moisture postures across each warm fleshy breast.

Awakening by the Cove

I delve into the velvet stroke of each
moan of each passing breath.
Softly, I dampen my pressing lips upon your pressing lips.
quietly, I return to the breadth of this fumbling silk sheet;
well into the hearth, I soak among your
warm bloods and the moan
of each soothing glance.

With the scorch of this Summer dance, I listen perfectly
to the feverish hour of flickering sweat, jousting upon the toss
of each trembling glaze, gloss.

I awaken in the press and glisten of
your tumbling lungs, breasts.
I enter the mesh of this cove, sauntering
crimp of the fall of the leaf.

In the freshest and first sting of morning,
I moan, saddened by the fresh harbor
which croons as the sobbing rains.
I rest by the water and awaken from each pulse of dream.

Covenant

I shook into the blush which threaded across the evening sky.
As the wind stood swift, I paused and cleverly declined
to the stone and pebble of the earth.

By the end of the scarlet dome,
I placed each petal of each flower upon my palm.

There flashed muds upon my heavy boots.
Gingerly, I lost my way through the covenant of the woods.

Buoy

In the deepest hour, I stood upon the mountain cliff,
bold and full against the threads of dashing wind.

I lean my head, open my mouth as a goblet.
The patter of the sweetest rains slipped and stung.

Floods of the trembling sea warmed within me;
I release myself to the sauces of the earth.

I hear the boats cry out for their harbor as each faint
smash of the buoy dances in the breath of nightfall.

Scarlets

With the strokes of the tree roots, I slumber.
Softly, I speak to the bloods of my ancestors which we share
upon this grove and vineyard.

By the next gasp and breath of the earth,
I soothe my way upon the fibers and
croon of these molecules.

Sweetly, I feed my beloved.
I fade to each stint of flash and croon of the light
which fractures upon the scarlets of the deep.

Burgundy Leaves on Meadows Edge

Through the carpeted gown, the burgundy leaves
crimp beneath the threshing spread of my feet.

I open my mouth and lungs and hush with each pasture
of the gluttony of deep fall.

I pause to see the patches of mint which floods my tastes.
gently, I open to the floods of this breath, dashing wind.

Into the fracture of Winter, paused as a lamb,
I stand beneath the threads of rain, trembling torso
and shuddering shoulders.

I recall upon the soils which pressed me forth,
I return to the grains and maize from which I fed my
ancestors and their cells and trembling molecules.

The skies open as a gash and thresh to the fields
where I roam and tread the coveting floods upon the earth.

Clusters

I carved my path across the fallen, tangled, tree branches.
Reaching to the shavings and buds, I listened.
I heard, gripped the sounds of every
wind and flashes of raindrops
which coursed through my shoulders and peaked
upon my calloused, blistered fingers.

Quietly, I placed my full, concave head.
I slept into the passages of last year at this moment,
the year before at this moment.

Now, I fell as dusts into the swooning winds.
I held the promise of the full soils
which pave way in mulches,
which spread to their tamping boots,
sweet treads of my children
and their children.

Into the scope of this endless woods,
I slow and sweep to the most polished bones
which quiver beneath you in dances of starry clusters.

Leagues Deep

The meadow hosts leagues of grape hyacinths
which toss fresh aromas across the
tuck of the Summer breeze.

I walk, pause, turn against the threading wind.
Knee deep in proud grasses, I
smile as the soft soil invites with an eager press.

I kiss her upon the indigo lips and sweeten
to every curve, both breasts and molding abdomen.

Upon the Earth

Each flickering lull of heavy chestnut hair
dashed across your sloping shoulders and wisped,
patterned along my quivering hands.

I walked into the slight press of yesterday.

I breathed deeply as the atmosphere brought you into my
full lungs and stamped you in each aroma of these
sweet passages of your tepid breath.

As I look to the sky which caressed you in flesh and full
swelling bloods, burning beneath the skin
as the snap of the apple and grape,

I turned and wept tears upon the earth.

Course of the Sun

I listen to the river as each thread and smacking water
chants and slowly lowers the sky.

The blossom fell in descent and coursed through the groan
of the dam and grip of the driftwood.

Over stretches and shattered courses of the sun,
I tenderly feed the roaming soils of the earth.

With the burning heat of the Summer,
crowning in posture and grazing winds,
I return to the endless dome of the billowing prisms.

Drought

I spoke and when I heard the murmuring winds,
I fell to slumber and deepened my flesh upon dry weeds,
onion shoots and sauces of the honey hive.

The bloom of the sulking skies breath,
scattered across my walnut colored hair, dredged along my
neck and stung my cottons with an open stitch.

After awakening, slippery drops of water beads
pronounce their title and feed their way along
open lips and dances of my leathery tongue.

I climb my way to the top of this earth
as gently, I stand upon this field, so
alive in moaning pleasures.

Cherry Blossom

I stood with arms open as a bantering crow.
Looking upon myself in the still water of the lake,
petals of the cherry tree fell, laughed upon my shoulders.

I took a breath and caused ripples in the now moving
spread. I tremble in the reflections of the panting sun.

Gently, I feed myself to the thick roots
of the bloomed, full tree.

Spade

As I dug my spade through the garden soil,
I paused, looked and found you.

Listening to the wash of the sky, I hung beneath you,
sipped the hottest of coffee's and sang sweet verbs.

You returned the song and tossed notes from this choir,
edging along in drips of the waterbead.

I stepped to the reach of the eaves and groomed
with sweeping gashes of wind.

In a dashing moment, the lemon sun
smashed through the clouds.
I returned to the garden and heard you sing.

Bloods of the Peach

In the sliced gash of the peach, there rose fumes which
coiled and trembled upon the spices of the earth.

I led my way through the humid wash of this
endless grove, quiet, tender.

By nightfall, I buried your seed and coupled with each fang,
dripping in this heavy flesh, soft and alive.

Bloods of your doughs perched upon my tethering fingers
and I split, fractured the floods of evenings rise.

She Posed as the Mountain

She carved her way upon the down pillow;
she fell into the dusts and full bloomed blankets
which glimmered from thin jaw line to the palest
of powdered breasts.

I stepped to the heavy seal, well gripped windowpane.
With the flicker of the snapping winds,
the bedroom became a fresh mountain lake,
a fresh mountain stream.

I knelt to the spiny, well shrouded creek and drank the juices
which fed the evergreen, coupled in muds
as each soft layer suckled upon my boots.

She stretched across my shoulders and back.
With each mumble of the fogs and tremble of the fallen sky,
she gleamed as a prism which cluttered along the flesh
she held in perfect posture.

Rivers perch before the fall of the rapids,
I recall swimming endlessly into the ocean cove.

Travelling East I Look For Her

Fabrics coiled along the trail;
I stretched through the thorn with patience
as I smelled the blood of her, dancing in the mulch.

Many moments ago, last Spring, her sparse, thin cotton shirt
lay as a gown, shuddering beneath her
as she flooded against me.

Now, I soak the clays and the hard earth,
dampening with the sauce of my flesh which
opened.

I wept for her as I travelled swift into the east;
the moon shook me in patterns of nightfall,
I fastened to the smash of the sun and called upon
her warmth which pulls me in sweat and burgundy,
wine colored skin.

Breeze

Approaching the end of the narrow path
which slithered through the hush of the fields
which waves of wheat as a full body, flesh of the sea,
I reached the most slender creek.

The red maple leaves fell upon each rapid and coiled
through the rippling dash of the thickening paste,
snatched by the roadside.

Here, I wept as the branches crackled in dominion.
I turned the width of my bust and heard
her upon the sweetest breeze.

Reaching the Apple Grove

Upon the highest ridge of the southernmost mountain,
I sank my humidity to the flesh of your apple.
Breasts of this juice of the earth casts me
in riddles, swoon of the falling
breath, perched upon me.

I rest from this climb until the fracture of daylight
softens upon me as I drift in scarlet.

I deepen in the wood of this bounty
which wraps each thread of the slumber.

Here, I sleep as the taste of her mingles
with the bloom of the shadow.
Well into the deepest hour, I return in the
soil, sweeping in dances and floods.

Scarlet Cloak

I wait here, alone by shadow, swelling drip
of the casket of nightfall.

The rains seeped into my mouth as I buried my frolicking
hands; I feel the oak leaves nibble upon my face.

Miles past, I hear the slanted gush of rain
slap and prune the eaves of my cottage.

I fasten to the muds of this small pasture
which pronounces each soaking edge of my nakedness.

With wind threading through the patch of trees,
I take leave upon the crunching pulse of each branch,
softly, I return to my cloak, heavy in the scarlet night.

Winter Veils

Scents of this Winter drift spooled and gathered in spices.
I placed myself in the walnut hues of your delicate eyes,
Soft veils of snow turned to streaming beads of water
Which threaded down the freckled chest, hiding
In the grip of your wool sweaters.

I took every scent of your flesh and slumbered
Within you as a gasp of frozen, breathing air.

I removed to the white garments of the pulse of the earth.
Softly, I treasured the pale breads of your fluid flesh, body.

As the stillness of the Wintery fields slumbered so near,
I trembled my way to the nakedness of your sauces which
Floundered from your cove.

I held the sweetest dash of sugars in my palm and
Turned your skin to fiery burgundy beneath the gush of the linens
And coil of the burlap blankets resting
Beneath your legs and waist.

As I Search for the Coast

With the dash of the blackening wings,
I listened to the feathers of the crows taking flight.

Leaning upon the base of the sweet cherry blossom,
crunching thresh of the leaves and enticement of the lime
green buds, I took slumber upon this earth.

As I awoken, I found myself in the deep of the valley,
shrouded in mumbling groans of the earth.

By the hours of nightfall, I walked to the glimmering
coast and drank with the seagulls and the ocean
which seduced me endlessly.

Pine Saps

The scent of the woods, hosting the
sting and sap of the pines,
I walked into the host of this spice
and fragrance, flooding me,
casting scents to the deep of my breathing lungs.

Upon this sultry encounter with the kelp ridden pond,
I slept through the moaning, dashing winds.

I returned to life with the gather of needles and fallen
mounds of the chipped cones.

With the crisp snap of the saps and clashing branches,
I stood and roamed across the fluids of the falling raindrops.

I opened the goblet of my mouth and fed upon the bloods
and flesh of this tenured soil and earth.

Creams of Your Breasts

I stand in the grooming rains which fall
upon me and I breath with the fevers of an oath;
the threads of the wool cloak soothe me in the birth
of sanctuary and crisp moisture on fresh laid linens.

I feed on the creams of your heavy breasts with charms
April just penetrated me in wines and bloods.

With the fevers of Summer's crimp and whisper,
I suckle upon the threads of an evening's pour and gush.

I fall with a swollen pouch in the flesh I covet.
I feed into the deep of tomorrow.

Conservancy, 2018

I return to the yellow and tan grasses which called for me.
The wiry growth of the regal triumph of the sycamore
swoons me in all trembling delicacies.

I stop and drink from the swift creek
where I dipped from and fished from as a youth.

By nightfall, I suckled upon the mint leaves and leaned
against the flesh of the earth and softly, I called to her

with the tremor of my heaviest breath.

Preludes and Fugues

Clouds parting and I cast my sight to the heavens
and witnessed the sliver of the sun.

Scattered patches of gravel strewn snow, I
fumbled my fingers and thumbs in
the wools of these pockets,

I felt the snapping sting of my toes and sleek heel.

The forest stood in motions of stillness
and stood quietly as a statue; with the
crackling pinch of the branches,

I watched the fangs of deep March press against the softness
of the rebirth of the soil.

Peering, gleaming the path of the sun
as it pounded it's way west,
I listened to the winds scream and howl
as they reached the woods
in preludes and fugues.

Summer Sleep

I witness the pulse of the slouching sun.
winds combed each beam and ray as I turned,
faced the rhythms of the passages of Summer.

Weeds and sprouting thickets wrench to the heavy
sky; sweat perches upon my lips.

Tasting the salts of the moan of the distant screeching ocean,
pampered in the softest of waters,
I quiver to the floods of the now star cluttered sky.

I wrestle myself from the baste and broil of a slicing slumber.

Each portion of you has fumbled in the pulps and salves
of my battered flesh.

From the sulking fade of the pinching sun,
I angle my grip and sweeten to the plump growth
of each Summer bulging grape.

Weeping in the Summer Woods

Upon entering the dark of the Summer wood, I
cloak my boots and denim of my legs, sweetly
with the groom of the thorn and
flavors of each snapping bud.

Upon the soft earth, I dreamt of sweet flavored waters.
Listening to the smacking crack of the branches,
looming in the treetops, I drift within the winds,
open with the scents of moss and heavy bark.

By the second turn of day, I
wept for the crisp dash of rain.

The sky smoldered upon me and I
dripped through the sleekest of parting water.

Slight Shift

I open to the slashing, pressing winds.
Resting upon the moss, grooming on the sleek rocks,
I dredged my palms on the pearls, white trembling dew.

High tide caressed me in sweet rhythms.
Well in patterns which carved their way through the strobing
turns of the earth, I slept beneath the moist soil
which soothed my flesh as Summer blossoms.

In a fleeting grip of ascent,
I danced upon the fabrics of the flickering breeze.

Apple Grove

I approached her in molecules which danced from the edge
of my tongue, sweetened fruits of an Autumn grove.

I drank the juice of the pulp and
chewed the wood of the seed.

Soft glances upon the swelling flesh of the apple,
I quaked to the smashing spirits of the fondling rain.

Standing beneath the eaves of the white, chipped shed
which shrouded me from trellising rain,

I asked her to cease and I soaked in the
soon, soft trembling raindrops.

Her breasts gathered and groomed heavy flesh upon me.

Curving Fields of Wheat

I listened, looked upon the cello which hung,
as the touch of you in all your nakedness.

You sulked and moaned into the cove of my ear.
I felt the tremors of the sky, opening as a prism,

dashing blood within me.

I roamed upon the swelling muscles of your thighs and groin.
I hear the flooding pasture which danced each stalk
of fullness and rhythms.

As I threaded my fingers upon you, I danced to the quaking
sounds of your voice, shattered in choirs and writhing wheat.

Forest Flood

Kneeling by the pebbled rocks,
I drank swiftly from the forest creek.

Floods of the icy threads
loosened into the deep of my throat.

As I walked along the wooded path, I
humbled by the freshest rain;
I stepped in the rippling puddles of root and fern.

Sounds of this moaning gown, greens and purples
cupped the dashing floods below me.

Dying in the Fragrant Air

Placed in the palm, cup of my hand,
I swooned, coveted the petal of the frailty of the orchid.

With a sweeping gash of wind, I loosened
and watched the white curving leaflet take to the breath
of the fragrant air.

In a dancing flicker, I witnessed the trembling, flashing
pond soak each rivet and vein.

Walking from this place, softened in the marrow
of each gust and heavy breath,

I took place to the drip of each cloud and soaked
in the cusping fog, soft about the angles of my flesh.

Nurse of the Valley and Woods

I kneel upon the endless wealth of the naked earth;
softly, I nurse with the groves and
their sweet nectar and pulp.

Turning to the blush of the warm
breasts, I soak in the murmur
of the pregnant hills, gathered with
pines and trembling evergreens.

Supple soils enriched and burning with the fever of the sun,
I dance through the emerald spreads and loosen myself

With flavors of the trimmed valleys
which soften through the breath
of the woods and all tendered mouths.

Lost in the Cavern

Caverns of quartz and smooth flaky slate
scurry beneath the stroke of my feet.

I look in response to the trickle of fading light
which deepens with the haunching shadow
which lurks within this heavy cave.

Pools and puddles of stale water tremble in the softest
dance and rippling joust from edge to edge.

By the seizing grip of nightfall, I
lost my way and groom through the passions
of the moist and dark.

Scenes From a Rowboat

I roamed across her flesh as the sun
against a late frost of a Spring window,
shouting in the murmuring blossoms, heavy pinks.

With an endless slice of the ancient, moaning rowboat,
I settled calmly in the blue dance of her cove.

Soft wind settled through our thin almond colored hair.
I felt the joust of her warm eyes and swiftly
I slurred my way across these breasts, buoys of the ocean,
trembling in groans with the spackle of the sun.

With the powdery fragrance of the garments cast asunder,
I entered her in the brine and sulking breath
which rivets each sway of the nearby cape.

Early Morning Light

Walking through the dusts of the slashing fields of wheat.
the oak towers in triumph of the trembling wedge and thighs
which contour to the supple stretch
of the earliest morning light.

Soft rain moistens the rows of dirt fastened to mud.

I gather her seeds by bushel and satchel.
I feel the warmth of her with the ongoing yearn of day.

She opens her lips with the parting sun.
I dredge through the fertile earth and flicker
in the dancing, drifting sunlight.

Infant Sun

I wade through the deep pools, fed by mountain springs.
Summer lashed upon the reds and ruddy
burn of my neck, shoulders and arms.

I open my eyes to the hush and graze of the heavy,
swelling pinch of the sun which lanced upon the earth
in falling ribbons, hosted the swelling birth of the infant sun,
so early in the smash of day.

I awaken with thirst and pucker my soft
lips upon the smooth water.
I drink the frothy, iced waters, now in the grip of Spring.

Sweetly there stings and stitches a time shift
As I flood my way through all days, quiet and soft.
All seasons calm and gush in angles of the swollen sun.

Waiting for the Falling Clouds

The freshly clipped pasture moaned proudly.

Yearning for the weight of the falling clouds
which drew forth water beads, slipping across
each spear and blade, I drank each pouch of moisture
which slipped into the brim of my mouth
by lips and laughing tongue.

I held the hand of the weight of the earth.

By pruning the swelling spread of the shrouding sky,
both moisture and hues of the color gray, I
wait in this gentle field and weep for
the sun to splash and tamp.

Daggers

As the garments shred, I discovered you in clusters.

I threw my fingers across shadows and gathered powders
which lay as the perfection of your endless body
and fevered flesh.

I sculpt you in fists and calm edging of the kneading dough.

Syrups gathered as a pond resting upon my loosened jaw.

Well into this moment, I lanced my eyes, flung like daggers
and faded to the tremble of your sauced and burning touch.

Farmer

I wade to my branched shoulders,
freshly dashed in grains and opening pods;
the earth crunched with every pinch and snapping step.

I breathed the cool air as it dredged through these warm
lungs which tossed flavors upon the rows of barley.

Moisture tossed into the air as fibers clung to the wools
of this jacket, sewn and hemmed, I
wash among the dances of the tossing breath of the emptiness
of Autumn.

With the final death of the suckling lips of this full
bodied field, I rest into new positions of the weave
of the grooming night's sky.

Belt of the Horizon

The posture of this ocean carved upon you,
quiet pulses, I fell deep within the softening brine
as fluids traced upon my lips and soaked the flesh of me.

Above, I looked to the canopy
which fractured the seams of the
threaded floundering clouds.

In endless steps, I walked to the belt of the horizon.
I grasped the leathers of my wine colored face.

These sauces traveled into the drench of night;
I gathered you in puddles and sang
tender vowels which soared upon the heavy mists.

Loose Petals of the Lilac

Wrestling my way through the maps of these roots,
softly the wind took a white shroud of a petal,
gingerly each rivet of breath danced; flag of the lilac
trembled upon the writhing creek.

Grasses wept with the flicker of the damp night's bloom.
now, the sweat of the Summer, deepening through the velvet
arching dome, walked the edge of this brook and listened
patiently as the beads of my flesh slipped
beneath the press of my lips.

Quickly, I angeled my way to the passage east and opened
my slippery flesh to the suckling touch of an eager sun.

Sweet Nectar

I stride through the delicate fog which wraps
across the earth, I feel the soft curl of my sandals.

Sweet nectar of the pines offers me slumber.

Stamped, the navy blush of the sky, perches dew
upon this needled bed.

In the faint quaking hour of morning, I
search this evergreen wood looking for a creek
which bathes the green sloping valley.

Funeral

I comb my path through the swollen dash
of the lush, winding river, soothing the mountains rocks.

I see a blackbird, perched upon a wavering maple tree.

I think of her as she would groom naked
beneath the blackened sheets.

In a current, fast moment, I absorbed
and pasted each slant of rain
as I tremble through this chill.

I watch the bird take flight and loosen to the sky.
As I weep in the pouches of my hands,
I can smell the earth which pronounces her in passions.

Awaiting Late Spring

As the girth of the sun fades and offers wet grass
beneath the waning light, I place her upon my lips
and taste a prelude of the most distant Spring.

Standing, looking into these empty woods, I smell
her spices which cast their way upon a snowy drift.

I spot her fangs, bleeding icicles which moan upon
the low lying mounds which starve each pouch of the grass,

Once loved in the long hours of Summer.

Spring bloomed late as I threaded
quick through the white gems
and hanging charms.

Reaching her cottage, I stood in mumbling
swoons of the earliest winds.
We undress for each other and warm
in stings and threads beneath
the wools of night's slumber.

I wrap in the hour of the long awaited breath of Spring.

Lehigh River, 1998

By the Lehigh river, the ancient trees toss vines and loosen
upon the jagged rocks, sleek on the water's edge.

The men boast their thick shoulders
with skin along their neck
sulked as a merlot.

I lean against the chipped bridge, chipped paints.

Summer sky floods in wools of gray as the rains
pat along the gushing water. Each riveting wave of the river
snaps at the flooding gash where this gathering will lead.

Heavy soaking cottons and flannels swish
beneath the tamp of the boot.

Tossing Shadows

The shadow I toss, falls upon your shoulders and neck,
the face of you and your hair, fullness as a waving tapestry,

I coddle the smallness of these hands.
sweet giggling carries upon the wind.

Well into the blankets of slumber, I
soothe the murmur of this
dashing, wrestling sweetness of dreams.

Quietly, I listen to the rattling windows as the row of homes
smash beneath the falling sky.

I watch you sleep as your bloods warm beneath the paleness
of your cheeks and pale arms, coiled
beneath your fumbling hair.

Rose Water

Sleek stones by the river carry gushing slithers;
the moss wipes clean as the kelp answers in retort.

Late Autumn, you perched upon the
climb of the Blue Mountain.
Waiting for you, I tuck beneath the eaves as I surrender
to the rain which carries the fresh scents of an evening mum.

You awaken me deeply, tucked in the folds of the afternoon
shaking clouds.

You wipe my weak body and gather the warmest wools
as I drank the rose water jarred last Spring.

Departed with the sobbing cloth which
caressed your bloomed,
full breasts and tense abdomen; the cottons
paste upon the floorboards
and I reach for you in this fractured moment.

I sleep and drift to the sweats of the river stones.
with tremouring joy, I step and wade through the kelp

Which tosses scents to the flare of my
trickling cheeks and jaw.
I wrestle through the swarm of blankets and soft down.

I glance upon you in the feathered bed,
softly in all humbling nakedness.

Sweet Petal of the Lilac

Her breath, sweeping along mountains,
tossed the sweet and fragrant
lilac, spread in the heaviest of occasions.

Softly, I slumbered by the piercing thrash of the pines
which tossed and wrattled saps and cones.

Feeling her cool, gentle arms coil across me,
I opened my cupped palms and drank each moisture
from the swab and coddled cotton, groomed,
this fog sulked across each shadow of
breast and curving pouch.

With the saunter of coming nightfall, I
placed a petal upon the edge of my tongue and laughed
my way through the wood and filtering stream
dancing along the mountains crest.

Honey Hive

Standing by the mouth of the river, I
coddle my senses to the dance of the honey hive.

I picture you swimming, slapping waters upon the twists
of your puckering flesh.

Hollow, the fog horns tremble through
the spread of the ocean brine.
I return to you at the casket of fading daylight.

Gently, you slither from the salted channels waters and kelp.
we walk along the mulches and soft soils of the path.

You smile and breath the honey in a trembling heave,
lifting and soothing the lungs she flooded.

Sweet Rain

I hungered, fed upon the mint leaves
and witnessed your charms as you
threaded, walked before me.

Wind lofted the fullness of your walnut colored hair,
crossed and bloomed full upon my face.

The soft flesh of you snapped in rains which thrashed
upon your apricot skin.

I felt the soaked sleeves of your arms which slipped
as a river.

Well into the heightened edge of this Summer moment,
parcels from you, I slept quietly upon you.

I awoke in the same precise moment, the same day.
I felt the floods of the earth adorn
you in pauses of sweet rain.

Returned to Maples

In all your youth and smallness,
I removed each root from the glen.

The sun sliced through the clouds and pressed
warmth upon the molecules, roaming through in dusts
and roaming seeds.

Looking to you with the sauces of each raindrop and flood
of the awaiting clay of the earth,

I swept my hands across the moss of you which
climbed the patient stones and bark.

Pinching you with the thumb and forefinger,
this pod, lime green and light and tender, I returned
to the stretching maples by nightfall.

Pale Flesh

With fog licking each blade,
I walked and waded through the meadows;
quietly I entered the empty woods.

Each branch and twitching twig, I
walked the earth which snapped
upon the frozen soil.

Having lost my way, I trembled upon a tree
and mourned the sting of the sun
which sulked in rhythms of absent posture and heavy velvets
combed through with the patter of the sweetest mist.

In this gentle slumber, I fade to the mountains
and reserve my flesh of the palest white.

Quake

Trembling canopy of the rattle and crackling branches,
snapped upon a gust of this mountain wind.

This wood stretched in emptiness as the moss froze
and glazed beneath the slippery ices where roots and mulch,
proclaiming purring rest and death of each twig, fell
to the gnarl of this white fleece, soft to the touch.

I spoke to the sky and heard no retort,
save the scowling wind.

Paused along the scattered cries of the frozen, frosted pond
I gathered a frozen nut and embedded it
in the deep of my pocket pouch.

Walking home, the winds chiseled against my molding face.
I fell humbled beneath the maddening quake of the sky.

Crows On the Lake

The kelp enticed, as the gush of the creek which swelled
and filled the patches of grass fallen to the edge,
the swish of the buried earth swept past the fresh
spread of moss.

I looked for you as the fullness of you belly
spoke to the fertile earth.

Deepened and ducked upon the soaked pastures,
a slight breeze tucked in the pattern of my eager ears
so filled with sounds.

Faint, the whistling hush of wind flickered through the trees
and moaned with each branch and tug of pollen.

I found you on the dock stretching
across the fat of this heavy lake.
You cried with the spirited, sour 'caw' of the crow,
so swiftly taken flight.

I rest my eyes.

Heavily, I dredge to the hollow of the wood.

Mother at the End of Day

I turn from this home, filled with antiquity.
The bones rest beneath the dirt sleeves of walls and roof.

I speak to her and caress her white hair with soft verbs
and heavy vowels.

Wind smacks every tremble of each
nook and splint of the frame.

You loosen to the hush of the loosened breeze.
Gently, I sulk to the touch of this withered hand.

Before this last lash of breath, I follow your parade of dust
which departs to the golden sun.

Moonlit Dance

Opened to the gape of your tender mouth,
I succumb to the treasures of this moonlit dance.

I groom upon you the meat of the swollen sky.

With the sweetest moaning of the puncture which tangles
me in lusty dances where we lull to the prisms
of this forbidden cast of nightfall, I surrender to you.

With the smash of morning, I tread my way through the jade
colored grasses and saunter into this endless probe of slick
glades which honor you in heavy pulses.

Well into this fractured morning, I call to you.

Doughs

I wiped the sweat from your gentle face, palm
to the rivers where I found you.

Fast, sweet waters tread upon the moss,
dying in the blast of the sun.

Humble, the creek sauntered in the crisp dredging glades
which covet these doughs of the earth.

I walk along you in longitudes and latitudes where
the soil impregnates and suckles tenderly.

Fallen Tree

With overlapping chymes of the wind
swept crackling branches,
I follow the music of these well forested soils, alive this
cluster, bunches of leaves dance before
us with wind and gaping breath.

I hear the snap of the red maple which threads upon the late
Autumn grass, deepened in a sulking
tamp of tan and heavy brown.

Resting upon this fallen tree, I glance with heavy blooming
starlight which tosses sweet vowels with
each mumbling molecule.

As I walk through this glamorous swollen patch of woods,
you breath the softest words in fabrics
of each crimped, crunched leaf.

Late Spring

The breasted hills roamed with pine trees,
jousting to the sky, lowering clouds.

I sat upon the mountain ledge, flooded
and alive with calm sloping rocks which took to trembling
dashes of fog.

Sweet dew, waters perched upon the blades as I
wept for the fevers of late Spring.

Calmly, I walked my way and found treasure in the collection
of needles and cones.

Reaching upon the swift water, I
I drank heavily and so gingerly, I thought of you.

Winter Day

Sunlight danced through the glint of the bay window.
I turned my head and in trembling joy; I
succumbed to the deepest day of Winter.

Birch

I soothe my eyes to the shreds and calm branches
of the birch wood, alone at the tender slouch of midnight.

I hear quietly with these leaves born for fasting Winter.
Well into the tremor of moonlight,
I carve my way upon the gathered snow.

As I listen to the passing breeze,
requiems fill the pockets of silent space.

Reaching my way to the wooded path of gnarled poise,
sweet, the choirs of the empty sky fills me in charms.

Fangs of Summer

In the stillness of the night sky,
I awoke and walked well into the fresh gown
of the puckering garden which swelled and moaned
in this birth of soil and dewdrops upon the leaves.

I dug my fingers across the fullness of my face.
the candle bled wax to the wood of the tabletop.

These fangs of Summer grew eager upon the sweat
cascading across my forehead and cheeks.

In the temptation of every pollen and swelling pod,
I turned to you and swooned upon
the gems of your soft face.

Summer Bloom

The glen grew in fevers as the soft breeze sweetened
each grass, alive as the victor of the Summer bloom.

Pollens swept across the fullness of each moaning field.
I dipped my way through the growth of the maple leaves
and the tossed sting of the onion sprouts.

I furthered my trek and rested at the
slice of the champion creek.

Tugging upon the rippling water, I drank into the dance
of the quick spread which yearned to
cakes on the pebbled edge.

Final Hours of Night

I rose among the marrow of the deep.

I spread in sauces upon you as you slept and soothed
beneath the draft from the slick, opened window.

You quivered in longitudes and latitudes on this silk
sheet, trembling in my groaning arms as silence crept.

As morning moments quivered and shook the tastes
of the passing sky, alive in the heat of this room,
full of preparation, I slipped to the grip of your sulking
shoulders and groomed the heaviest of words.

Past Peak of Night

In this trembling hour of dark,
I opened the grip of the lusty breeze and deepened
with the shouts of the moonlit shades.

Soothing my way across these sweet and sharp linens,
each stitch and fabric burrowed in the spread of my chest
and shimmering thighs.

Daylight brooms the wooden floor;
I carve my way to the glimmering dusts of morning.

Lost in the Dash of Water

I touched your slender arms and the sky opened;
grays and marbles shook through the field
which groomed to the heavy wood.

I stood nearest the reach of the tremble
of the heaviest evergreen.

Rains pounded the soils to sulking spreads of mud
as the deepest pouch held each casket of water;
upon walking my way to the pinewood forest, I
shook in the drip of the tears of a frowning blast.

Reaching my way to the forested grip,
each pinch and dash of water trembled from your full breasts.

In the evening hour, I lost my way.

Wood Chasing

Breathing the whispers of the blushing winds
which coil and thread their way upon me;
I sink to the earth in vapors which freshened upon the lake
and danced through each tree, alive in the wood.

Fevers flashed across me as I moaned for each
pleasure which trickled along the poise of my trembling flesh.

I found you in the hollow where the wood tosses
each scent and groom to the pastures of your breasts,
sloping abdomen and fiery thighs.

I deepened into the heavy woods which softened
to you again; alive in the quake of your shaking cove.

You came to me in prisms of perfect light and dampened
the edge of my brow and curling fingers.

Weeping for Daylight

The sky dripped to the earth and swam
across this woodland trail.
I paused upon the approaching bend and followed
the coil as each whipping branch shook
my shoulders and arms.

Fewer steps and I reached the calm
poise of the quivering pond.

I met you in the edge of this pouch of the earth
as the kelp and lilypads danced before us, clutching
each breath with the verbs I sweeten to your grooming lips.

From the fangs and vapors of the swelling sky, I
wept for the cringing passage of daylight.

Walking the Fields I Thought of You

I swam through the voices of my legs
grooming the fields of wheat.
With boots tamping the crusted dirts of the earth,
the rain began in rivets and puddles upon the slender rows.

I opened myself to the sizzling sun,
pouncing the treads of water and poise of the perfect bead.

As the flair and open pods which
tossed grain upon the wind, I
thought of your hair grooming the
sway of the chisels of my face.

Each flicker of rain water cooled the
sour burn of my Summer face,
Summer arms cast the color of burgundy.

Heavy Sun

Now August, I shouted my path to the sun.
Verbs of light flickering upon the passing dust, I
angeled my way to the soft beds of spreading grass;
With this perfect softness, I dug my
toes through the quiet fields.

I spoke to the clover and in quiet retreat, I
paused and searched the dancing meadow.

In tenderness, I stopped by the passing creek.
Stopping in frequence, I turned to the bloom of the sweating
glimmer of the heavy sun.

Journey

I chiseled my path through the heavy stalks
looming to the breath of each glance of each soft wind.

Swooned by the dance of the spread of the onion sprouts, I
dipped my legs through every patch of crimping grass;
I walked in the trembling sway where blooming breath
from the sweats of the sky fell to my flesh in beads.

The trembling pines which dashed to the sky
and threaded upon the distance of the clever mountain,
I found the spiny creek and drank deeply.

Beyond the joust of mountain to hill,
sweet words of the endless forest glazed
across horizon to horizon.

I trembled my path through pine cones
and beds of soft needles.
by the end of day, the sweet winds passed through the glaze
of the fullness of my hair.

Warm Blood

I carved my path upon you with tremors from the Summer
breeze tossing across the breadth of your breasts
and all their fullness, filled with creams and spooling milks.

With all cleverness, I thread my fingers through the silks
of your hair.

Into the dancing depth of nightfall, the
crickets fondle constant verbs
through each pocket of cascading darkness.

I sleep upon you as the rivers of your warms bloods
pulse within your flushing flesh.

Jade Hue

I slept beneath the velveteen spread of the heaviest night.

Soft strokes from the trellising breeze coddled
each bead of sweat and pulse of the warmth which deepens
within the posture of my moaning flesh.

Breathing the sweetest answers to the questions
of this burning Summer night, I retort
with the perching breeze which humbles into this fragrance
which soaks and dampens upon my flesh
and all it's quiet madness.

With the smack of the morning sun, I
sleep in the groves of the softest beds,
jade hue of the humble grass.

Summer Walk

Rains soaked swift into the clays of the earth.

I breathed the perfumes of Summer;
I breathed the trembling sauces of this evening grass,
quietly alive as the blades holstered
the beads and trickling press
of my tamp of the nakedness of my feet.

There spread wealth with the swaggering
dance of Summer's night.

By morning, I vanish to the buds and quivering pods
alive in the sway of the softest sunlight.

Open Sky

I wept with the dry clutter of the dusty earth.

You pressed your breasts to my mouth and hurriedly
I dredged my fingers across the beds of your thighs,
shoulders and abdomen.

The sky swelled and sank in rhythms as the rain soothed
the caked beds of this garden grotto.

With the strongest of winds, I return
to the soil from which I came,
dusts upon the open sky.

Coursing in Scarlet

The breath of deep night courses across me in scarlets
draped from the sky as the fallen clouds swab
both vision and my dancing flesh.

Quietly, I think of you as the rivers of my forested dreams
dash and flood the dipped swoon of flesh and foot
upon the suckling sands where I once waited for you.

Breeze and tucking winds tremble upon the sauce
of my soaking skin.

I awaken in the heaviest of flight which roams
across me and pauses with the first glance of Summer's end.

This fleece of my dancing sight opens me to rivets
and curls; The sauntering press of Autumn clings,
the glisten of daylight opens agape.

Winter Fleece

The dome of the sky grew swollen,
moaned with every moment, fattened with each
thread of a stitch of a darker hue.

I lulled beneath the fragrance of the Autumn
pinch, the crisp scent of wilting leaves.

With brief passage, I found myself in the stretch
of the pine woods, suckle of the sweet saps.

At the precise second, next year, I suckled upon the vowels
which throbbed and smashed through the threshold
of Autumn blushing to the fever of scowling winds.

Now, deep December, I trembled in the screaming winds.
the last of the maple leaves toss to the fevers of a frozen
fleece, grooming white wintery beds.

Red Maple

I dwell through the night in all antiquities.
chipped nuts buried in the hardened crust which
rests in slumber with the burrow of the earth.

Once fastened leaves, strapped to the quiet growth
of the red maple, loosened to the breeze which
returns in multitudes, threshes in garments on the trembling
blush of the quiet dirt gown.

When morning slices through in slivers, passing through
the scattered clouds, I gather my thirst
and take it to the stream.

Hurriedly, I taste the freshest spring which
treads and spools upon the stream coiled deep in the valley.

Well asleep, I gather among the shreds of the burgundy leaf.
the soil softens in anticipation.

Flock of Geese

Wavering branches and delve of the empty root,
I smell the perfumes of the latest moment of Autumn
which suckles the scattered frost, opened to the clutch
of surmounting wintery glazes.

I gathered the iced chipped nut which freshed beneath
the first chymes of the fallen snowy pressures.

Into the thrashing arms of heavy January,
my brethren pine lulls into a heavy sleep, tenderly alive.

With patterns of powders fresh upon the white snowy beds,
I walk upon each signature where the flakes rest,
threaded as the softest quilt, the sky screams in ices
with the sweet and belated flock of geese sauntering south.

Flooded, the earth opened each chiseled spread,
the combs of the oak and dance of
the maple tossed the scarves
of Winter into the abundance of heavy screams.

First Perch

The trail to the mountain perch breathed sweetly upon us.

I traveled west and soaked the frailty of my lungs to the
thinning sparse avenues stroking each tender grove,
countless pouches and pockets of the douglas furr.

Each needle curved from the base to the tender tip.

I found the mountain spring which fed all grooves of water;
tempt of the pond, lake and swerve of the stream.

I drank and felt life source through my blood.

By rocks and moss covered stones, I
wept upon the shards of ices which freshen and began

upon the perfect moment of sauces and showered boldness,
alive and antiquated.

Autumn Trek

Grass snaps beneath the bareness of my heavy foot.
In the garden, the pond proclaims of stillness and shouts
of the slithering green kelp.

I rest upon the smoothest of sleek stones
which host the moss and gather the water bead
as the creek dashes past.

One second past and it blooms the colors of Autumn
as I walk through the fields and thicket, I soothe
my way along the wheats which tremble upon the wind
which dances against my buckle and waist.

As I breath the fragrances of the humble snip
where the mint leaves flush upon an open breeze;

Fresh dance of the scattering dust flounders
across the sour aroma where the earth suckles
the marrows of the buried rib and follow every
curb of the horizon.

April Sky

Leaves of the sycamore and nearby maples,
loosened upon the cool, chilled breath of the snapping
jaws of each near Winter loft where I walked through
the beds of soft snowy white.

I reach into the softest powders of snow
which piled along the curve of the creek.

I placed a pinecone in the pocket of my denim.
By Spring, dusts flew to the April sky.

Dusts and Pollen and Broken Pods

The lilac whimpered upon the gales of Summer ghast.
With dreams and a temporal bloom to the uneven sky,
Seeds and broken buds danced into trembling passages
Where dusts reign triumphant.

I step upon the burning soil.

Into the wealth of the richest minerals and regal mulch,
I feel the leathers of my feet return with the soon
Arrival of my legs and whimpering waist, well into
The pastures and porridges where I covet the earth.

Meadows Flood

I speak of service as the rain waters
thread upon the low spread,
Arrivals of each trembling voice, the
meadow courses through,
The jade glen blossoms to the laughter of a soft wind.

I wear each pouch and patch, thicket and
weed, as the thunder humbles itself
In rhythms of a gentle gift.

Well into the dredge of the midday sun,
I pause with each slap of rain;
The dancing bloom suckles upon the
breadth of this Spring dance.

Sweet vowels whisper and crimp with the floods
Of this labor which crawls to me in peaks and ravines.

As I tremble in the sauces of the sweet
joust of Spring dampness,
Ankle deep, I roam through the pasture of meadows flood.

Thornbush

Fastened to the grove of the thornbush,
I slivered through as the beads
of blood postured upon the thighs, hamstrings and ankles.

With drips and punctures, I spoke of living and the servitude
which fastens to the flesh of each threshing
body, so alive with pulps.

Fresh rain pampered to the earth and flooded in the deep
of threads of blood as the denims and cottons I wore
paused upon the needled and stung fractures.

Soft speech, I listened to the hush of the soothing winds.

By the depth of night, I slept into the carved doughs
which rose and fell as the grip of this Summer swelling flesh;
I spoke to the chaos of this thrashing field.

Among the Heather

Softly, I walked among the heather;
soaked, I drank the sunlight
with the tremble of my Spring flesh.

I found passage in the trail, fumbling upon the glint
of the brook.

Moans of the pasture filled my lungs with dry pollens
as the stroke of the mustard seed buried
upon the shake of roots.

Gently, I sat upon the smooth reaching rock,
stretched upon the jettison across the drifting water,
slants of moss covered the slippery reach of the stone.

I knelt by the wayside and drank the icy threads
which fractured the heat of my flesh, beneath my abdomen.

Eagerly, I captured the scent of the drifting heath.

As I wade to the waist in the smacking dance of the water, I
tremble at the waves burning in an icy touch.

Hemlock

Walking into the depth of the heavy woods,
I glanced upon the hemlock and burrowed my way forward
as the gentle patter of the rain shifted the clay earth, moaned
into suckling verbs of the thread of the stream.

I turned and looked back as the water hemlock
grooved into the marrow of the northern reach.

Walking past, I smelled the rib of the earth as the moisture
of the trail, rose in fragrance and blushed upon the legs
which trembled past, opening avenues of a swallowed prism
which slickened through the gentle sky.

I heard the drip of the leaves of the poisoned plant.

In the Cove

The bedsheets moaned as you tucked and harbored
among the dancing, floating dusts.

Resting among the down covered bed,
the islands rose and fell,
deepened in the cove you sauced with supple care.

I removed the sheets, garments and cool, crisp silks.

Looking upon you, lulled to the wavering of the buoy,
I sulked in rhythms as the fog horn undressed the sleek
waters of the fondling harbor perched beneath you.

Softly, I reached beneath these linens and tugged forth
in thudding veins and slapping eddies upon the shore.

Burgundy Leaves

Upon awakening, I found myself in the
deepest stretch of the wood.
Threaded leaves of burgundy and fallen leaves of tan,
A trembling white gold, gathered upon the press of my feet.

The high top branches rattled with the
banter of the sour screech
Of the black feathered crow.

I tore the mask of the earth and lay
upon the dew covered moss.

This forest stretched to the rise of the pine covered hill,
Stretching to the reach of the pine covered mountain.

Gently, I breathed the soft of the earth.
I wedged upon the slice of the permeating
saps which burrowed through
Each rivet and valley of the crimson covered leaves.

Chip of the Bark

The clouds of South Mountain fell and
thinned their breath upon the earth.
Well in the pockets of my lungs, I breathed life.

The fog crept to the basin of the valley,
crept as a slithering serpent
tugging at the tightening throat and chest.

Last year on this occasion,
the spruce tree wilted each shard of branch and bark.

This year, the same moment,
the spruce tossed each chipped fragment of bark.

I rest on the perch of the lake, rising
the grooves and path where the coddle of
the waves muscle across the edge.

Morning fade the fog and tilt of the mist.
I return to the spread of the heavy late Autumn day.

The forest trail rises as the clouds fall;

Mist licks the mountain in glazes.

Sweet Aromas

I listened to the howling ghosts as they
spun threads across my flesh.

Sweet aromas of the lavender bush and peach tree
flooded and filled the grotto where I
last touched your full breasts.

As I walked across the bloom of the grass and soft moss
where you lay for me in tangled threads,
I dampened the smooth
pearls of dew and placed a bead upon my tongue
only to taste the persperations of your gentle neck.

Alone, you are a phantom lurking in the hollow of my bones.
as I approach you, the words fall apart and I
speak to you in moaning howls of vowels
which suckle upon my lips.

Waist Deep

I awoke, witness to the trimming edge of twilight.
Purples and fading apricots dove beneath the horizon
past the creviced peak of the mountaintop.

Here, I stand in the field of wheat, overabundant waist high,
grooming grasses which toss at my cool, cotton shirts.

With this fading dance of daylight,
I soothe into the moonlight and suckle the near honey hive,
blooming about my face and passing in a soft breeze.

With this mad gust of sweet winds,
I return to the quiet, pampering shiver
of the fade of softest Autumn.

Apricot Flesh

Sauces tremble at the flesh of the apricot.
With each snap of the jaw, I taste the perch of the sun.

Walking swift, I fasten to the threads of grasses
and loft of the searching thicket which tosses spurs

Upon the motions and burrow of the flickering dance.

Night fastens with the tight thinning
stretch of the drum, the wild
thunder of this Spring, each early Spring cascades across
the belly of the purple sky.

From the pouch of my satchel, I fill
each corner and socket deep with the
skins and aromas of the nectar
which bulbs and fattens loose upon my tongue.

Ponds From the Heavy Gales

Scattered ponds shook to the wrangling course of the sky
Which lowered and thinned, fogs upon the soft films.

I soothe with the nakedness of my body
To the naked skins of kelp against kelp;
Quietly, the drenched sauces of mud
Suckle upon the deep of my feet.

I remove myself from the green waters which flaunt
In silent dispersion and moan with
The crackle of the sacred night.

Slithering fogs wrap me in the gauze which dampens from
The heavy mountains stapled to the northern gales.

Maps of the Oak

I expose the trembling, flickering dash of light
through the dancing tree limbs, past
yellow and burning leaves.

The oak, scarred with the map of the
young, the map of ancient
tales of roots burrowed deep.

I paused as the earth deepened beneath me.
The threads of an iced cold stream flashed along the soothing

valley which tunneled across the heavy kelp.

I turned my head, looking to the spread of the woods.
Calm and softly, the light softened
across bloomed and carved
endless threads of forest light.

Empty

I soaked upon the narrow ledge where fading
Moonlight deepens beneath the summit of the Blue Mountain;
Softly, I hear your breath which sulks on the grooming
Press of the sweetest breasts, sleek upon the grassy hill.

Blood of the earth proclaimed in moans as I tucked
Fragrances well upon the socket of my lungs.

I drank heavy, the milks and thick creams you blended
Upon the floods of the valley;
Softly, I rest to the mountain face and sweetly,
I opened my eyes with the rise of the sun.

With these thick trees of the forested wood, I gathered
Each pulse of musk and thread to the silence of this empty forest.

Milkweed

Lips flicker upon each wavering crunch of the milkweed,
dance of the onion root which pause and covet
the grains and fields of the earth, alive in these moans.

I look to the canopy of these towering woods.
light of the fading sky lessens and softens upon
flurries of pinks and heavy purples.

Sweetened life burrows through the tastes of the honey hive.

With the snap of the grooming woods,
I opened my hands as a goblet and fall to her in a stitch
of the garments you loosened to the
crunch of the wooded floor.

Fangs of August

Against the quickness and fury of the hot Summer winds,
I lent my eyes to the charcoals of the midday sky.

Feeling the pulse of the dying clays of the earth,
my flesh gathered sauce and softened the dance of my flesh.

My body spoke in each leathery hue as my neck
sizzled the patches of burgundy and I moans through

each scream, tumbling across the deep of the rains.

I howl through the fullness of my mouth, lungs.
each drizzle upon the mud of the mulch,
I coil in the treasures and charms.
Wild, I stood to the soaked grip of
August and all of August's fangs.

Silence

This marrow bled in thick salves and sweet nectars
as the juices flood upon my body which shook,
drenched.

Here, I give this gift to the pulses of the perfect field.

Gently, I return myself in quivering shards and moist
molecules as I quiver upon the thicket and fruit bearing tree.

At last breath, I hear the threads of water
trickle to the mast of the maize and stalk of wheat;
I tremble in silence.

Arrival of the Sun

Beneath the sober perch of the sober sun,
I removed myself from the cotton shirt;
I swam in the gusts of this breeze and softened my flesh
to the fingers of this rising peak of daylight.

Walking by the roadside, I deepened into the woods.
Quiet threads of the trembling leaves and gathering
of the humble spread of pine needles,
shook me loose and burrowed aromas which suckled
swift upon my gentle fine threads of hair, shoulders.

I stepped each foot after each foot, I felt the pillowed softness
of every moss.

The days grew endless as the sun returned in the pulse
beneath my skin; I humbled in these flushing bloods.

Bare Woods

I removed myself from this body, coated in flesh.
Tenderly, these aromas buried in musk
shook the vowels from each sweet sentence which
dripped from the slant of my mouth ajar;

Heavy verbs and snapping consonants coated me in shrouds
which suckled the breath I took, threshed in vapors.

Quiet, I tangled upon the death of the empty field,
the naked shout of the bare woods.

I threshed my passage and ginger walk as I stepped
to the edge of these poisoned trees, alive in the venom
of Winter.

Cherry

Between finger and thumb, I pinched the pale green bud
Which snapped into life and smothered the bloom
Of the tender fragrant breeze.

My naked feet slipped through the wet coat of the patches
Of sweet, tender grass.

By the rise in the dome of the naked flesh of the moon,
I knelt to this thread of this creek.

I drank as the seeds from the cherry tree soaked dusts
Upon me and layered my shoulders and back in films.

I am the moist soil beneath the dipped roots beneath the
Towering stretch of the great cherry wood.

These leaves are the nakedness which coat the flesh of this bark.

Glaze of the Peach

I wait, until morning, when the sky coats
the peak of South Mountain,
soft glazes of peach.

The earth spoke to each tamp and press of the boots
which groom the soil into a launch of fertility.

Paused at the quiet pond, I look upon the silks and kelp.
I recalled the breath of her as fog upon the soft waters,
sweetly, I recall her nakedness.

Surrounding the pond, I walked through
the grass and thick weeds.
I see the breasts of you, pulse with glazes upon the edge
as water roams across the pond, so covered in lace.

Shoreline and Seagulls

I place my palms on the curving shoreline of your waist.
Reaching to the ocean of your smooth, soft abdomen,
seagulls whimper in the curl of your voice.

Beneath the heavy waters of your sleek, simmering bloods,
I fasten to these ribs, moaning beneath the dunes of your
creamed breasts.

I place the warmth of these hands upon the slithering
floods of fog, having crept from the fallen sky.

Phantom

There moaned phantoms in the bones of antiquity.

I angled this hickory cane against the mound of soft grass
and I leaned to the bark of the wood and slept;
I loosened to the winds and flurried with
scarlets of this slippery night,
dews softened upon the carpets of grass, weeds and thicket.

I feel the age of descent climb across me
in ribbons of the moonlight.
I hear the speech of the nude trees, stamping the avenues
where Autumn fades.

Soon the forest will empty and leave
all skeletons of the woods
alone in all nakedness.

Softly, I mumble with the breath of the scattering wind.

Cocoon

I wrapped you in warm cocoons.

Placing you upon the needled bed of pines, I
trembled within you as the sauces of the rains
pamper through the slices of late Summer.

Mosses and ferns groove upon the carpet of the earth.

I unfold myself and slant to the tangerines and apricots
which shake from the softness, falling quick.

Beneath the slant of the warm sky,

I awaken.

Tenderly, I soothe from these dreams.

White Petals

Pines thread the river's edge;
Jousting, the clouds falling sparse and thinned.

Fine indigo water swerves to the distant lake,
Surrounded by the surmounting hills.

Soft, the azaleas perch white fumbling petals
Which spool and dance the river's coat.

I open myself to the mouth of the groomed, tender wash,
Supple waves of the lake.

Inch after inch the eddies of the fastened sauces
Which thresh beneath silent breath, curve to the stretch
Of this sweet, green, rising hill.

I turn my face in a glance and soothe to the edges
Of azalea bushes, tossed in whites to the rivets of this tender lake.

Spring Hue

The flaxen hue of the April sky shed soft light
upon the stretch of hair, silk across her shoulders,
past the curves of her threshing, wavering back.

I reached my way through the grooves and sway,
alive these fields of wheat.

As this rain shouts and flickers soft dusts,
each meandering cloud, fattened to the course patterns
of gray and black the sour sulk of charcoal.

In the dance of Spring next year, I
wedge my way through the dry snap of the buds
which pinch upon the wheat.

I wander tight and place my hands upon you
as the brisk dash of yellow rumbles across the sky.

Coats of the Earth

With temptation of the blooming warmth of the open
sun, I walk in treads to the east, pause, then west.

I am the sorrow of the crimping grass
and fallen fleece of leaves
which scatter as I loosen upon the wind.

With a shout of colors, heavy pinks
and indigos, I slither across
the mass of the peak, alive upon the mountaintop.

In an instance, I cast my hues and colors of sweet burgundy.
The sweep of the ocean washes upon threads of me,
washing in endless waves which yearn for my sanded floor.

By the casket of night, I soothe, humble and naked.
This soft cloak spreads in navies as brine
and the freshest of mountain air

polishes each step where my feet coat the earth in sweetness
and floods the sky in tapping cool breath.

Morning Blackbird

With the softest tremble of your flesh,
Heavily coated in fresh tans and the sting of the crimson
Which smooths to the freckled chest, deepened
To the breasts which saunter in the perfect fragrance,
I swim across you in thin cottons and sweet gauze.

Upon awakening to the blackbird at morning light,
I reach upon the waist of the waist of this down bed.

You fade in vapors and slip
Through crackling edges of the wall.
You swiftly seep through the bay window, open ajar.

Clinging to the sulking blush of this bed, I
Breath the aromas of you as I fade in every direction.

Hunting North

Plucking roots from the dark minerals of this deepened
sulk of fertility, I
knelt upon the spread of emerald moss and breathed
the scents of my ancestors which hold dominion
over the threads of the soil.

With calm breath and steady feet, I rejoice in habits
of the passage of this blended gloom where the sky suspends.

Tapping rain swiftly salves the hot of my flesh.
I retreat to the deep of the wood where
I surrender the sweet lush
of the grooming mosses.
Eagerly, I search for the chill of the north.

Lost in the Frozen Wood

Frost assembled along the spiny creek.

Upon kneeling to the freeze of the mosses,
graded with the sleek stones, I
drank swiftly and felt the blades of ice seethe
down the edges of my throat.

I fastened and sank the wedges of my boots
as the lusty winds burrowed through the soft
woods.

In the perfect moment, I witnessed the chimney smoke
which unravelled through the birchwood and the hickory.

Lungs freshened to the corridors of the sweet winds.

Jasper and the Meadow

Beneath the fallen branch, shavings of bark,
the jasper revealed itself and shook to
the glamor of the treasured
sun. Softly, I placed the history of the
earth, delved in the pouch
of my pocket, grooved as the goblet of my curves.

Inscribed upon the pale yellow of the
quivering stalks of the meadow,
I watched the pollens take flight and
loft in garments, only to settle
and remove to the rock laden path and cling to each branch
of every tree.

Across the breadth of the field, I tossed the stone to the well
breasted mound, curve.

With the glaze of the burst of the pods and buds,
I felt the tossing seeds mask upon my
face and I walked swiftly
into the woods and found passage to the
tumbling rapids of the stream.

Eulogy for the Autumn Rain

With fine drizzle and silk webs dampening upon me,
the fade of her cotton shirt and soak of her denims,
I heard the moans of the fallen sky.

From breasts, to curve of the waist, and flicker of the thigh,
I turned to her in musks of the gripping soils;
quietly, she left with a tender stroke of the nearest chapel
which unfurled her to the waltzing winds.

I breathed her in spreads of the spruce and mumble
of the walnut as she sank to the trembling
cascade of Autumn earth.

Winter Incense

I host these blankets of burlap and pillows.

Each thread of the quilt layers upon me as I tug for
the scents of your almond hair and perfumes of the
sloping shadowy breasts.

Into the silent stillness of your shoulders
and soft nape of the neck,
I hover across you and breath incense which tosses across
both room and fabrics you adorn.

I listen to the pamper of the snow
which grips and coats the window ledge.

Searching for the Death of WInter

Past Autumn and the tangled woods slept dormant.

Rapids of the swerve of the creek sauntered to a halt
and moaned of the stiff ice which soothed in hollow tears
at the height of midday, the blossom of this Wintery sun.

Into the passion of the crisp chill of the slicing breath,
I stood among the death of the branch and root.

Alive in the empty woods, I sauntered to the chasms of this
stretching pattern of white.

Looking well into the distance, I see
the vapors of the nestling
screech of grasses blooming in emeralds and soft jades.

Eagerly, I slave to the taste of the pulsing sky
which taunts in the tightest of rhythms.

Silent Melt

The sky once opened in swivels and screams.

Walking through the silent melt and mesh of the earth,
shedding the powders and trembling
mourn of passing snows,
I tread, wade upon the blooming tears
of the flooding meadow.

Soft, the quilt of the bedding of the well speaking earth,
threads of the earliest green, I watch the bud thicken.

With several strokes of the sun, these
buds scattered about the twigs
and joust of the branch.

The fleshed bloods of frozen patches which fed the roots,
deepened in fiber and growth of the melted snow, I
fell gingerly to the passages of grooming Spring softened
my rest in the hammocks of the dashing canopies of this calm
feed, the breast of the arrival of the quivering sun.

Blood of All Seasons

I spoke from the shroud.

Quietly, I shouted silent verbs and vowels
As the passing field, sulking wheat, pronounced my descension
To every white groove of mineral and black
Softening yield of soil, treads of clay
Upon the quickest speed of approaching Winter
Rose to the edge of the thin trail, rows of golden, dancing buds.

I shook the earliest Winter glaze.

With the speed of the smacking beds of white mounds
And the freeze of the snarling wind which dashed
Each caress of powdered touch of the earth and all flashing flesh,
I fed the frozen muds of the meadow; I sank in all
Humbling silence to the iced patches of Winter and slanted
To the rise of the Spring, slow groom upon the earth.

I am the blood of all seasons.
I thicken and thin with the passage of the sun.

Patience of the Bud

I peak and twitch upon the reach of the pale green twig; I
fold and quiver to the first breath of Spring.

Beneath the winded gales of the spoken bloom of heavy
March, I lean to the passage of April.

By the fresh sting of the spears of May,
I pierce the fluids and saps
of the surge of the maple and the triumph of every
rise of the pine.

Silently, I severed the swelling pouch of the bud.
Calm powders and dusts took swift to the sky.

Waking Early

Tender to the slapping waves, softened shores adjacent
to the salted edge with dusts swelled upon the muds
and silence of the slippery moss, I hear the gentle pulse
of the heavy reds and gentle pinks of the opening sky.

The slowest blitz of the flesh of the horizon,
I glaze my trembling lips and quivering fingers and thumbs.
well within the passages of passing morning, I watch
the yearning of this slippery dome.

With shuddering glimpse of the garments which sweetly
fell to the earth, the floods of the cove,
I felt the dancing waters
and the moan of the laborers of the water, quickly fill.

Fractures

Within the chasms of the coolest touch of your icy strokes,
to you I hook these coiling toes and
deepen my crimping palms
upon the laughter of the wind which slaps the slippery
fade of these relentless windows.

With an adornment of the breath I
sauce across your warm breasts,
I shout a silent moan as the perch of your burning thighs
melt the chill of the perching heavy quilt.

With the opening reach of the fall of Winter,
I view each stalk and thread of the fractured Autumn
which fell to the haze of frosts and dripping fog,
ash gray clouds.

I speak to you of fractures of the
madness of the sleek wavering
earth.

Well in the depth of the freeze of your slowly melding fingers,
I leave this home and walk through the fangs of your garden
and iced crackling grotto.

Walk in the Earliest Autumn

Treading through the green meadows, I felt
the grass curl beneath the edges of my naked feet as the soft
wind soothed across the fullness of my chestnut hair.

With the shaking draft of this early Autumn glaze,
the cheeks of my face and crimping sting which rounded
upon the reds of my hands, I shook the winds so deeply
into my breath.

Reaching the top of the crest of this hungry, starved peak,
gently I lean against this silently moaning oak tree.

After a brief fraction of the most gentle time,
I stood and loosened to the further
tempo of the rising winds.

Tenderly, I threaded with the bareness of my supple
walk and reached the breadth of the swift, roaming creek
where I drank and found the pinching ripples and rocks
pulsing this coursing blood through the
fondle the heightening breeze.

Necessary Morning

I stood by the willow tree which slung
and wavered as a ghost,
soft fingers of a trembling phantom.

By nightfall, I slumber and quiver to the most eager dance,
alive in this mourning toss of a heavy breeze
which burrowed into the moans of my saddened face.

I stood among the branches and cast my sight to the fire
of the rising plateau of morning.

I stood and walked my course.

Hot Breath

Summer gales rumbled through the once stiff pierce
of the grappling pine.

Needles tossed through the ruffage of the earth,
so alive in chipped nuts of the sweet cones
which fumbled across the soil and above the deepened roots.

I stood upon the jettison peak of the edge of the cliff.
Looking upon the blackening sky, I begged for the hot breath
of the churning soak filled clouds.

In a moment, I smelled the sweet dash of the brine filled sea.

Moaning Treasure

Well before the age of my youth, alive and deeply placed
in the soils and trembling from the grains, I
swept to the gems of starlight and cast
my fullness to the fertility
of tender eggs and minerals which soak upon the moist clays
of a damp and rich earth.

Born swiftly into the treasure of her soft and majestic floods,
I felt the warm burns in her blood and spoke
to the polished drenching and eager pronunciations;
I reached for the fountain of this moaning pause
which reached my pursing lips upon the glaze in the quickest
feed of the surface meeting the brim stance of suckling life.

With the farthest moment in reach, I
fell aslumber to the reach of the endless wave of wheat fields
which toss the burst of the pollens and greed of the bud.

I sank my teeth and fangs to the soil I love.
I soothe and sink to this moaning treasure.

With the most tender touch of a passing leaf,
I dance to the threads of this tumbling sky.

You will find me in the cakes of this moist earth, so dismissed
to the crevice and lofting winds.

Walnut

I removed these drafting, drifting scents from the honeyhive.
My feet dredged across the cool, soft moss which soothingly
welcomed and spoiled relentlessly.

I turned my face to the sun and felt
the warmth of the endless
rays burning upon my face and neck,
alive in wines and burgundies.

I swam my way through the first second
of this enormous Autumn
display of leaves showing the bend of
tans and the glaze of orange.

I awoke several times as the smack of
Winter pinched upon the
edge of my approaching crisp sting
where flesh burns in the dash
of snowy mounds and beds of white.

I fall in the torrent as the walnut chose a
fastened grip, well into the deep
strangle of ice and fever.

Along the Eastern Flank

I dip my legs through the thicket, lilac
bush and coat in the regal
crowns of the lavender bush.

I read the southern skies as they reach
the spread of the eastern flank.

With tender covet and wild prune of the thorns,
the preserves of the heavy sky tangle in
deep reds and wild purples.

Clouds thinned and threaded across the
smooth southern mountain,
I hear myself in echoes as the cliff top demonstrates.

As I return to the thicket, lilac bush, and lavenders so alive,
sweet moans of the warm winds,
throttling the evenings dome,
I feel my flesh dash across the northern peak.

Tulip Tree

I rose to the leaning peak of the tulip tree.

Every dancing flicker of petal and twig
so softly discovered me in the depth of the most gentle graze.

I swiftly groomed and gathered the perfect lumber
as the tender emeralds, this full grass, coaxed me to swarm
each sprout in heavy vowels.

Across the wax of the stiff Summer spear of grass, I
knelt to the earth and breathed the smokes of the madness
of every spark of the crackling fire.

Maple

I wedged my fingers and thumbs swift into the deep
of the rich garden so filled with mulch and minerals.

Upon finish at the fattened edge of Spring,
the weight of the pulses, tenderly stroking within the earth,
I groomed the green sprout and the dance of the moan
which fastened to my flesh and smiled,
stroking me in rhythms.

With the quickest lights of morning, I
swam through the floods of the pink madness on the edge
of the pregnant sky.

The jousting pen of the lumber of the earth,
I leaned, slept upon the base of the sweetest maple.

Openings

Gathering a scattered flock of dusted leaves,
as they bloom across my flesh, tender upon my arms,
soft grip of my face,

I awaken to this fastened tremble of morning light.

Sweetly, I take to the open sky.

Hook

Well into the silent freeze of the heavy,
shaking, smash of Winter,
my toes hooked, neck and face burned in ices as I dove
through the temperate arms of Spring.

I took to the soil and burst into
shattered flakes of frozen flesh.

In a dash to the tremor of the chiseling sky, fallen
in ribbons of sleek, tender fog, I gave myself to the gardens,
the remote, yet open fields.

I watch you as you snap the stem of the tiger lily.
I soften with the breath you gather and watch you as you step
upon the my ribs and softened clavicle which still
croons to the maw of the past Winter sky.

Through Creek to Meadow

The pinks, indigo and almond trim clouds
danced through the vast dome of the sky and bled in fire.

Salve of the soft whimpering creek swelled to the banks
and called me to wade gingerly and naked through the soils
which suckled my feet and ankles.

Looking through the fields, acre past acre, I
swung my arms in all conviction and swept
through each groomed thicket.

I loafed beneath these fastening hues and trembled
to the shaking draft which stopped and drifted to the shaves
of this meadow.

In a moment, I withered and screamed the gestures of night.
with a ready return, I swam through
the deep channels of the gentle

creek and found myself lost by morning.

Dash of Dust

The cherry tree bloomed in pink flakes
which fell to the ground,
blended in the graze of emerald upon the grasses which
bent from the rich soils, tender to the pause of rain.

I leaned, loafed by the tree and watched
the pink blossoms scatter across the asphalt
and tangle in the youthful twigs
of the earliest sprout.

I hear the screams of the deepest root.
Silently, by the edge of the last shaking winds by the moment
past the edge of the bloods of the earth,

I blushed and tossed upon the breath
of the sweet, white cloudy sky.
I return to you in a dash of dust.

Mountain Escape

Beneath the soaked, hot sweat of the sky,
flooding the deep of this ancient forest,
I slipped through the branches and flickering shrubs.

Quietly, I felt the thud of my coursing bloods.
Gingerly, the crows took to the treetops and sang the chorus
of this canopy and webs which thread in hammocks.

By the stem and twig of the floating, moving creek,
I wade in all the nakedness which groom both tangling kelp
and the spirits of the soaked soot
which suckles upon the ankles and coarse heel of my feet.

I wedge my way to the towering Blue Mountain;
I walk through the pine beds and broil beneath this steamy
lowering clouds.

Life Lesson by the Hickory Tree

Leaves upon the hickory tree
waver in unison as the flags upon the nearby, stretching pole.

I caress the smooth, wooden bark
as the slippery mosses tangle upon the basin and floor
of rock and routing roots.

Turning to the joust of the quiet spring,
I knelt and drank the blue and white flickering water.

In sketches, the tangle of the thicket and underbrush
scathed upon the naked wedge of my feet.

In seconds, I heard the crackling branches of the hickory tree.
I heard the slap of the northern winds which danced
through the threads of my full, moaning whisper.

In the Grove

Reach to the fullness and ripe bursting skins,
alive in the swell of the plum tree,
I feel and drink the juice as the gush and stroke
threads upon my cheek and loosens upon my tongue.

We leave this sweat filled grotto,
alive in the smack and quake of the needling sun.

I reach for the moisture of the sweat soaked breasts.
into the distance, I hear the blackbird sing.

Posture

Dead leaves and this shave of the spear of of the floods
where the maples trembled naked and the roaming gesture
of the mountainside stood empty, I
filled myself with the fragrance
of Autumn and all broomed dusts which
coated me in fleeting pollens.

Standing upon the steepest peak,
I leaned in perfect posture, softly I looked upon the glazes
of the snapping fields and their pinching cover of frost.

With the whiplash and shake of the wild winds,
I felt the dampness of my clever blood which filled me
in gentle burning veins as I reached to you and coated
my arms with the crushing spread of this icy wash.

Secrets

Between the flicker of the clover and the gushing
water of the creek, shrouded in pines
covered in leaves of the forgotten maples,
I soothed the ache of my now nude feet and sweetly,
I wade through the channel with pebbles beneath me.

I loafe my breath through the crackling branches.
I wedge my way well into the deep of the furthest woods.

I stop at the patches of the wild hyacinth
and tug each snap of spice
as I covet this soft, blooming place.

Drying my tender feet, I groom near the
ancient secrets of the sycamore.
As I tremble, soothe and sulk,
the dancing rains soften the earth and
moan upon my crinkling flesh.

Well Suited

In flavors of the shave of the wood,
modest greens plumped in lime buds upon the ancient tree.

I gathered a well suited stick and
declared this motion, my staff.

Gently, I faded to fogs and dampened in mists
as the webbed reach of the field tucked
and begged beneath me.

Flash

I feel myself drip upon the hot burn of the asphalt.
Weeds wiggled through the slice and crack.

I look to the once empty sky and glaze myself
in rains now falling as the blankets which shroud you
and complete the sweats upon your cottons which
soak each swab of your breasts.

I return my face to the marble sky,
flooded in dark charcoals and occasions of the eggshell
clouds, groaning in the whimper of the approach of absence.

Return from the Mad Summer

Leaving the graze of the slapping, drifting winds
I fell fast to the floods of the dark, mourning forest which
slumbered in the breadth of age upon age.

With a slight lift of the gown of this peaked and roaming
woods, I stood motionless and watched
the curve of the meadow
as the melt of these winds triumphed in recurring rhythms.

I softly admired the rooted fangs of the softness of each
starved and thirsty tree which deepened forth and suckled
the sauces of the Summer and Summers madness.

By twilight, the oranges and pink
stretch of the moaning navies
in the evening nakedness, I walked through the forest.
With emptiness in my hollow, I returned
to the meadow I adore.

Winter Walk

I step upon the shivering grass and snap the frozen
threads of the weeds, alive in the stiff earth, frozen mulch
of Autumn.

Sitting by the iced edge of the stream, I slung the flattest
stones across the blue water as each
toss flickered by the red chipped paints of the bridge.

These boots crimped and shriveled as the sour
deceased fields moaned with the stretching glaze of a soon
Winter is arriving.

Reaching the shaving whites of the home,
I lulled in the heaviest of blankets and soothed my flesh
swift into the tepid wrap of the feathered bed.

By morning, I reach for the pulps of the fat of the tree.

Woodland Walk in Winter

Sparse grooves of scattered January
grass became stiff, crippled
as the branches of the birchwood tossed and flung from tree
to birchwood tree.

Sulk of the frozen draft slanted the willow tree.

As the harbor of the icy tangled air pelted the canopy
of the soft treetop, I turned and walked to the meadow
and field of wheat which faded to the white caps
of the freeze of the earth.

The home stood in all ancient wealth as the soft snows
toppled across every slate stretch of the rooftop.

By nightfall, I slept in the dredging covers and blankets.
Patterns and stitch of the burlap brought me to the distant
moans of this Spring.

Ice Fading

Icicles of the branch, drizzling in soft drips, fell
as fangs to the sweet pampering snowbeds.

Reaching the wilt of the twig, slung upon this tree branch,
I gently placed the lime green bud between the pouch
of my finger and thumb.

With the deepest of breaths,
I chiseled my way through the mumbling moans
as the wind cascaded through every motion of every tree.

The sun danced through the pass of the clouds.
I turned the polish of my face to the heaviest smash
of the early Spring grooming.

With decisions of this blooming patches of grass,
I wedged my foot upon the open glare of the fading
snows embedded upon open fields.

Alone with the Pulps of the Apples

Into the dense Autumn breath, I walked
through the width and length of the remaining stitches
of the grass coated apples which soften in the sweetest pulps
and soaked the edges of my throat and gums.

Winds trembled in waves as the sculpt
of my walnut colored hair took flight with these
chilled coatings of scent and drifting spice.

With fleeting muscles and weakening knees and snaps
of the branch beneath my feet, I
felt the press of her breasts against the softening creams
which tread along my mouth and lips.

I watched you wedge your way through the trees
as I loosened and suckled my way through the softest earth.

Garden and Glen

I soothed across the bed and nested along the down pillows
as the hot linens glistened sweats and thickness
from the width of my groin and the pulses I conquered
well within you.

In passions and glazes of the steam trickling along the bay
window, I sulked across the tension of
her ribs and smooth abdomen.

Morning, I stand alive in the sweet garden and glen.
I walk through the opening charms of the pine woods,
I continue through the crest of the endless horizon.

Mints to Pods

Sleeping among the well cared and
well groomed leaves of mint,
sweet tremors of grazing breath dredged across
the softness and contours of my face
and the sparsely bearded neck
danced along me in minuettes.

I fell upon the heavy leagues which swept in patches
of grass and waves of each sprout.

I felt the dusts toss beyond me as I shook
the velvet coat of the sky.

By this nightfall, several decades upon decades,
I crumble and snap beneath the groves hidden in the earth.

I return to you as a budding pod grows upon a sapling twig.
Soaked in the gusts of the patient winds,
I dance upon the breadth
of each passing breath, alive and spry.

Roaming Fields

The tender wind pressed upon me as hot linens and moisture
from the soaked nape of my neck.

Kneeling to the orchid, I rushed every droplet of blood
sweetly upon the tangled earth.

By nightfall, I return to the suckling breast of winds
and gasping waves.

I walk the endless roads of the eager countryside as each
vapor roams to the softness of low lying fog and suckle
of the green carpeted grass which lay in bundles of blankets
of quilts.

Rest Within the Pines

Upon the syrups of the wavering pines
and all crackling branches,
I stooped and slept as the leaf of a passing maple
landed and rested upon the peak of my trembling shoulders
and I announced each dash a grip of
the wild, wind of Autumn.

With sweet posture of the tossing needles,
I fasten my head and neck upon the mosses and draped
my torso through the snicker of the washed, waving ferns.

By morning, I look to the grooves where I humbly slept.
I face the reach of South Mountain
and slice the curving wind
as every shattered and chipped cone lunged beneath me.

Gazelle

I cross the rock hardened earth, swift as a gazelle.
The pulse of the sun thickens the flesh of my neck
in the drip of burgundy and my arms as crimson.

Well into the forgiveness of the fattened forest, I
pause at the silence of the blue pond which trembles on kelps
far beneath the surface.

I drink the warm water heavily into the caverns where
I coat and crave.

I look to the girth of the swelled and moaning woods.
In a moment, I dash to the deep.

Winter Path

Having furthered my way within the ginger touch, powdered
beds of white, I feel the icy burn upon the hook
of my toes and sting of my calves.

Into the gathering of the carved stretch of the trees,
I lean against the birchwood and dream in the pastures
of Spring and all limes and emeralds.

I awaken to this icy fleece gathered around the soft glen,
postured in the thick of the forest.

In a rock hardened flank of ice,
gently, I tremble to the humid course of my breath
and the dead staves of maples and elms which fastened
to the crimp of suckling roots.

In the fraction of a tender moment,
I hear the moans of the rib and curve of the clavicle
burrowed beneath the earth.

Slowly, I walk upon the cakes and tortes
of the soothing snowbeds.
flakes gather in the slippery groove of my hair, beard.

Resting into the stiff neck of the tree,

I breath the frozen air.

About the Author

Donny Barilla, a poet covering the realms: human intimacy, nature, mythology, theology, and man's relationship with death and the departed, has been writing for over three decades. He writes daily and strives to renew himself as an artist from page to page and body of work to body of work. Very seldom does he take a break from writing as he views it as a full-time job. He lives a reclusive lifestyle and finds himself clinging close to nature and all her elements. His home state of Pennsylvania strikes chords of poetic depth about him as he finds loveliness from cornfield to meadow. Whether it's feelings of love, intimacy, or a special closeness, he maintains the feeling that death does not take these with him/her to the grave. Emotions and feeling outlast the flesh of the human body. Human intimacy draws near an enigmatic spiritual passion which conquers all on the prismatic scale of experience. When speaking of mythology Donny says, "myths were created to make sense of feelings which are complicated by very nature. They are perhaps more easily understood through persons greater than oneself. As for theology, a disciplined aspect, incorporates quite finely with passions and secured poetic comforts.
https://twitter.com/BarillaDonny

www.ingramcontent.com/pod-product-compliance
Lightning Source LLC
Chambersburg PA
CBHW032225080426
42735CB00008B/720